T0196680

VAN *of* TRUTH

R.K. DEMENT

authorHOUSE®

AuthorHouse™
1663 Liberty Drive
Bloomington, IN 47403
www.authorhouse.com
Phone: 833-262-8899

Published by AuthorHouse 08/04/2022

ISBN: 978-1-6655-6627-8 (sc)
ISBN: 978-1-6655-6626-1 (e)

Library of Congress Control Number: 2022913711

Print information available on the last page.

Any people depicted in stock imagery provided by Getty Images are models, and such images are being used for illustrative purposes only. Certain stock imagery © Getty Images.

This book is printed on acid-free paper.

CONTENTS

As I walked around the van I read the big yellow word. MARANATHA. Yes, that and various other bright-colored religious slogans; ONE WAY, JESUS LOVES YOU, ONLY THE CROSS, and TRUTH, were hand-painted on the side of our recent purchase.

In years past it had been seen in motion on the streets of our little town. A sort of mobile kaleidoscope in search of passengers;

now, only occasionally would you see this bold machine. Many of the older citizens of Broseley, Missouri must have thought it pretty ugly.

Those words; Pretty and Ugly. How do they fit in the same sentence? They are of opposite meanings. One sugggests (I do believe) pleasureable or appealing to the sight. The other would suggest non approval or un-appealing to the sight. I have heard it said that, "Beauty is in the eye of the beholder." Well, now my family beheld this beauty. One must be informed that it was the late 1970's and all those blue, orange and yellow colors; the ugly, from previous years stood out!

I however, do beleive that God loves our

'Pretty' by looking past our 'Ugly'. He sees us for what he created us to be and he loves us despite our flaws. The deciples had flaws and yet, Jesus understood and forgave them. He continued to use them to build the church. We have to realize that they knew very little if anything at all about Jesus when he chose them.

Ugly was all over them when they left everything to go with Jesus. He looked past that and selected lost individuals to train and fellowship with them. The men he selected began to go through a life-changing transformation.

According to Ephesians 2:1-18 New International Version our true repentance gives us a new life. The change may take a while, but it can happen when we agree to allow God to work in us. A much-needed transformation begins to takes place.

With all our ugly washed away, we become beautiful. Romans 3:21-26 reminds us that God made us to honor him through his son Jesus. We deserved death, but God's grace allowed us to live a new life. He loves us just as we are and calls us beautiful. After true repentance, the way we bigin to live out life should represent our change. Don't just speak the Biblical words, but live them out.

Big flashy words are nothing if there is no proof of a heart change. God wants our hearts first. After that the rest can be cleaned up.

Although the words on that van had truth in them, they were just words if they did not reflect the action in the lives of those who read them. The Bible encourages us to show action in our Christian walk. We need to get rid of the dirt that hides our new heart That, I believe is true and why my dad constantly encouraged my sister and me to let our lives reflect Jesus. We struggled with this through our teen years and into adulthood. As a Christian adult I am checking myself daily to see if my life reflects a relationship with Jesus.

2

The year was 1978 and I was a nine-year-old boy in love with all kinds of automobiles. About this time I had begun to collect Match Box Cars and Hot Wheels cars. I also had a few scale plastic models. I could identify several brands and models of cars and trucks by now. My dad would often quizz me by asking me to identify a car as it drove past. I began educating myself in automobile history.

I did this by reading books and magazines about the American autombile. As I got older I developed the skills needed to build scale plastic models. So, I have to ask myself and you how much we realy know about our Christian history and the Bible?

Do we study the Bible? Are we reading to gain information on living Christ-like? Much like my newly found interest in cars, we should be always interested in knowing the gospel of Jesus. Many times, when asked, I could give the year of the car as well as the brand. So, when we are quizzed about the Bible or christianity can we give an answer? Our interest in God's word should excite us.

It should consume us just like a kid obsessed with the history of cars.

You can imagine my excitement when I saw this oddly painted van that now sat in front of our house. I slowly studied this as it sat in our drive. I admit I wandered what went into the artistic design of this van. How did the artist or artists come up with these bold phrases and bright colors?

3

My dad had just purchased an old 1966 Dodge
A-100 van from the Baptist church. Just in
case you are not familiar with these, let me
describe them. This thing resembled a toaster
with wheels. Dodge built these compact vans
and trucks from 1964-1970. The one we had
was flat-nosed (cab over engine designed) and
full of windows. There was no interior to speak
of and the ride was rough. The driver actually

sat over the front wheels and the in-line six-cylinder engine was hidden under a metal box between the two bucket seats. In the back were two bench seats bolted to the floor. Two double doors on the side allowed access to the bench seats.

Think of the Mistery Machine from the 'Scooby Doo' cartoon. Only our recent ride was covered in bright-colored words of religious slogans and it stood out! It was obvious that the youth group from the Baptist church had designed and hand-painted those bright colored words. In years past it had served its purpose of transporting the teens to and from church.

Everyone new that van. In fact, our town was so small we knew most people by the car or truck they drove. When a vehicle drove up to a business during the week or for church on Sunday we just knew who it was before anyone steped out.

Sadly, the Baptist youth group had dwindled in size and the van was no longer needed. This often happens in small communities. The youth graduate,leave and their place is left empty. It is difficult to grow a youth group in a small community with several competing churches. There has to be a program that is new and relevant to reach them. So, for whatever the reason, this youth group had shrunk and the van sat rarely used.

My dad and Reverend Gene Langhoffer (we knew him as pastor Gene) were new aquintances who met through their respected proffessions. Both were ministers and each drove a school buse for our educational district. Now pastor Gene was one who liked to take the gospel to the streets. He played the trumpet and his favorite songs were "Amazing Grace" and "When The Saints Go Marching In". He would stand in the parking lot of the local bar and play as the customers arrived. On several occasions he would enter the bar and hand out gospel tracts (pamphlets). He was not shy about Christianity.

So dad worked a deal out with pastor Gene and aquired the van. He came to the conclusion that we could use it for our family camping trips, hauling things, and even picking up souls for our little church if needed.

The church we attended was Broseley Church of The Nazarene. A blue sign with white lettering had been attatched to a white post giving notice to that fact. The building was located on Highway 51 that ran thru town. When we first came to town we lived in the attatched parsonage (small living quarters) at the rear of the church. You could walk through an adjoining door leading from our living room into the church. No excuses for being late to church services. We later moved across the road to a two bedroom house on a hill. The back yard sloped steeply for a few feet then leveled out before stopping at a shallow bar ditch. I learned to ride a bike by rolling off this hill.

4

Broseley is a rural farm town, located near the southern tip of Missouri in Butler County. A quiet little town with minimal traffic. Back then things were pretty simple. There was no cable TV, internet, cell phones, or game systems to keep us busy. We had to ride bikes, pull one another in wagons, and various other outside games or activities. I spent many hours outside while growing up.

A few homes and churches dotted the land scape along with a limitted selection of busunesses. One single stop light hung above the two-laned crossroads of Route 51 and Highway CC.

Missouri's smaller roads are identified by letters for names. You could cover the alphabet by driving through Missouri.

Speaking of names. Lets take another look at that van. Maranatha is an Aramaic term that means " The Lord is Coming." When I look at Matthew 25:31-32 New Living Testament and again in Luke 12:35-38 New Living Testament I find the promise of Jesus' return. I do not know the day or the hour so I need to be living like he could show up anytime. Do you live as if Jesus could show up any minute?

Although my family and I believed that statement from Matthew to be true, we decided that it and the others were a bit too 'in your face' for us. It was going to be our family vehicle. We were repurposing the van. It would be given a new identity.

You see, my dad was pastor of the Nazarene Church that I mentioned earlier (a new pastor) and he did not want any confusion as to who or what church now owned the van. As I said, everyone knew who drove what vehicle. So, we removed those bold statements and gave it a coat of grey primer. It now became our second family car, the camper, and sometimes, the church bus.

I remember spending countless hours helping strip the paint away. Being a young kid, I could only be of use scrubbing and scraping from about the bottom half of our new project. This could be compared to Jesus removing the rough spots or the ugly in our lives. He begins to transform us into something new.

There is only one way to get rid of the ugly and get to heaven. John 3:16 informs us that only through Jesus can we get there. We should get our hearts cleaned up by accepting his love and correction. We have to be willing to go through a change.

5

At some time during ownership, the van needed an engine overhaul. Dad gathered help from a couple of men from our church and got to work pulling out the tired engine. During this process, we managed to break the windshield.

Mistakes would be made and corrected before we were finished. Just like the van, we may have several areas that need work. We will make mistakes while we work on cleaning ourselvs up.

God understands our human weakness and that we make mistakes. In Ephesians 2:10 We are assured that God continues to fix us and use us for what he intended. We will never be a finished project but we will be complete in his eyes.

The father and son team who helped had, on several occasions, worked on and collected various cars and trucks. I do beleive they worked on just about anything with an engine. Glenn and Kerry Payne would drive some cool and interesting automobiles. Oh, I loved going to their house to see what they hade parked around the yard. Sometimes a Chevrolet Camaro, a custom van, a dune buggy or on one occasion a motorcycle. You never knew what they had. Their shop was always full.

6

Dad fixed the windshield and got the van running again. He was handy like that. Most of my life dad could be found imersed in some project. He had a tallent for fixing things. I don't know if he did it beacause he could or because he wanted to save money. Either way, Dad was constantly building or fixing some thing. He could take a few peices of lumber and make a table, a cabinet or bench. One year he made mom a dining room table and a china hutch from oak plywood. They were beautiful.

Now that the van was fixed we could go on a camping trip like he promised. We used the van to go visit family in Redford a few times. The trip north would take us through the lager city of Poplar Bluff and the wooded country side. It took us about an hour drive to get to grandpas farm. The trips to the farm were great but nothing like going to the river.

I rember a trip to Centerville to take the family camping and fishing. We filled the van with boxes of camping supplies, bedding, food, fishing tackle, and other odds and ends. I just knew this was going to be a great trip.

We had been to Black River several times

and fished from the shores and gravel bars. Dad had grown up in this area and was familiar with the river. Upon arrival dad began to look for a place to park. There were no designated parking areas. You just found a spot and set up a camp. He viewed others parked on those gravel bars and decided we could do the same. He drove onto the gravel bar and before long we were stuck. He tried and tried to get out but eventually we had to get help.

After getting pulled out, we managed to enjoy the rest of our weekend under the summer sky.

I still enjoy camping and fishing. Our church does an anual camp out at Beaver lake. When we have evening services the music echoes accross the lake to form a beautiful sound. We get to worship God within his wanderful creation. This becomes one of those great opportunities to erase all the worry and fear and be in his presence.

I have had times in my life that I thought it was safe to do a thing and then I found myself in trouble. My bad decisions caused me to look to God and ask for help. I get to talk to him, worship him, and be reminded that I can get help in times of trouble.

I do not remember catching any fish on that trip, but I am sure someone did. Fishing was one of my dad and my favorite past times.

We only had that van a few years, but I can

still picture the grey primer and two bench seats.

I was just a young kid Of nine and my sister was seven. I have always been interested in old cars and trucks. I guess that is why I remember events involving automobiles. I can always find a connection to my past and our family's modes of transportation. More importantly, I found a connection with God and his word thru this van.

Printed in the United States
by Baker & Taylor Publisher Services